THE KVELLER HAGGADAH

A SEDER FOR CURIOUS KIDS
(AND THEIR GROWNUPS)

ELISSA STRAUSS   GABRIELLE BIRKNER

ILLUSTRATED BY HANE GRACE YAGEL

CONTRIBUTORS:

John S. Allen
Rabbi Joshua Cahan
Amy Cohen
Hadley Creighton Bergstrom
Rabbi Sari Laufer
MaNishtana
Ruby Namdar
Rabbi Ruti Regan
Rabbi Danya Ruttenberg
Laurel Snyder
Nanthia Suthana

Kveller | *www.kveller.com*

ISBN: 9781090974839

WELCOME TO THE SEDER TABLE

WHY.

This is a word kids use a lot, right? Kids, raise your hand if you use the word why a lot. Why so many whys? Because "why" helps us understand why the world is the way it is, and sometimes it leads us to how it could be different.

So why are we here tonight? Well, kids are probably here because their parents said so, and their parents are likely here because the Torah said so. Every year on Passover, Jews are supposed to gather around the table and remember the ancient Israelites' escape from slavery a long, long time ago.

The Israelites — what our Jewish ancestors were called — used to be slaves in Egypt, forced to work hard, day and night, for no pay. There was no way to escape, until God intervened and brought the Israelites out of slavery and into freedom. We call this journey the Exodus.

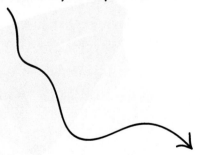

As the Torah says, "Remember that you were slaves in Egypt and that the LORD your God brought you out of there with a mighty hand and an outstretched arm."

The Torah commands us to remember, and the seder shows us how to remember. Tonight, we are going to talk a lot about what that means. We're going to talk about the importance of memories: making them, keeping them, sharing them with others. Memories of things that happen to us, like our first airplane ride or our last day of summer camp. And memories of things that happened to other people before we were born, or before we were old enough to remember.

What happened to our great-grandparents — or to the Israelites who left Egypt — didn't exactly happen to us, but we carry their memories with us. We are the keepers of memories. It's our job, and it's an important one.

In fact, memory is such a big deal at Passover that we actually eat memories. Really! See that seder plate, with all of its colorful foods? See those little dishes of salty water or vinegar? Those are memory foods. They are here because on Passover we don't just remember with our minds, we also remember with our bodies. We're expected to do more than just imagine what the journey out of Egypt felt like. Tonight, we're supposed to feel like it's actually happening to us.

Parts of this long meal might seem downright confusing. But that's the thing about the seder: You are supposed to be confused! And then you are supposed to say to your parents, "Um, what in the world is going on here?" This is because Passover is all about asking questions, and we're not just talking about the Four Questions that you may have practiced for tonight. If there's something that doesn't make sense, just ask! And that goes for everyone around the table. Some say that a seder can't really begin until someone asks a question.

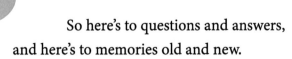

So here's to questions and answers, and here's to memories old and new.

Because tonight we aren't just remembering, we're also creating new memories. Years from now, what will you remember about this very night?

HOW TO USE THIS HAGGADAH

We created this haggadah to be informative and spiritual, and even a tiny bit weird. We think you will love it, but we don't expect you to read all of it. Well, at least not in a single seder.

This haggadah is for families, and because families are all different, it includes lots of different ways to move through the seder. It's not a traditional haggadah, but we've got all the important elements — Four Questions! Ten Plagues! — along with lots of other readings. "Memory Lane" contains short explainers about how memory works, and "Top Secrets of the Seder" looks at the juicy parts of the Passover story that usually don't make it into the haggadah.

How long you want to spend on each part, whether you want to pray in one or more languages, and which of the extra readings you'll discuss now and which you'll save for another time — that's up to you.

We hope that as the years pass, as you get older and your curiosities shift, you will find new ways to use this text, while never forgetting the very old reasons that brought you to this table in the first place.

MEMORY LANE:

How Do Stories Help Us Remember?

Every year, we celebrate Passover to remember how God led us out of slavery and into freedom. How do we do this remembering? Do we do it by studying maps, memorizing dates, and taking quizzes? Nope. We do it by telling stories.

Stories have a special power. When we hear them, our minds try to relate to them. If you tell me a story about something that happened to you, it will probably make me think about when something similar happened to me, or a time when I felt the same way. Many times, I will respond to your story with a story of my own.

In this way, stories build on one another. Other people's stories become part of our story, and our stories become part of their story.

This happens when we talk to one another and when we read stories, too. Think about Moses, Pharaoh, and everyone else we will hear about tonight. When you hear their stories, do you try to connect them to something you have experienced in your own life? Who does Moses remind you of? Who does Pharaoh remind you of? What does it mean to feel free? We will all have different answers to these questions.

Someone once said, "A writer begins a story and a reader finishes it." Every single person who reads a book reads a different book, because we can't help but mix our personal stories with the stories we encounter. This is why stories mean so much to us. They don't just give us a chance to learn. They also give us a chance to connect.

Source: Laurel Snyder, writer and the author of "Baxter, the Pig Who Wanted to Be Kosher" and other books.

SEDER PLATE

Zeroah (זרוע)
Although the lamb shank bone — or a
chicken bone — doesn't play a major role in
the seder, it is a reminder of the animal
sacrifices the Jews offered God a long time
ago. *Zeroah* is Hebrew for "arm," and it is also
supposed to remind us of the "outstretched
arm" God used when taking us out of Egypt.
Vegetarians and vegans in the house? Use a
red beet instead of a bone.

Maror (מרור)
The bitter herb, commonly
horseradish or romaine
lettuce, recalls the bitterness
of slavery.

Karpas (כרפס)
A vegetable (frequently parsley or celery)
that we dip into salt water, according to the
Ashkenazi tradition, or vinegar, in the
Sephardic tradition. The greens symbolize
life and renewal; the salt water or vinegar
represents the tears of the slaves in Egypt.

Beitzah (ביצה)
Boiled or roasted, this egg represents the animal sacrifices the Israelites offered to God on holidays, including Passover. Its rounded shape also symbolizes the cycle of life.

Hazeret (חזרת)
A second bitter herb is another reminder of how truly horrible slavery was. Some say we use two bitter herbs because one, the *maror*, is supposed to be eaten on its own and the other, *hazeret*, is supposed to be eaten as part of the Hillel sandwich, which you will hear more about later. (Many families use *maror* for the sandwich, and that's OK, too.)

Haroset (חרוסת)
The sweetest thing on the seder plate, it is a stand-in for the mortar the slaves used to make buildings for Pharaoh. Its name comes from the Hebrew word for clay: *cheres*. Some families make it with apples, nuts, and wine. Others make it with dates and a variety of dried fruits.

Tradition Additions
The seder's host may also place other items on the seder plate. An orange, for example, is a sign of LGBT inclusion. A banana represents support for refugees. You might also see a pinecone, cashews, olives, or fair-trade chocolate alongside traditional seder plate staples.

Passover Used to Be Very Intense... and Bloody

by Ruby Namdar

Today, Passover is nice and calm. But it wasn't always that way. More than 2,000 years ago, there used to be a massive, beautiful Temple in Jerusalem. Every year, Jews from all over would travel to the Temple right before Passover with a lamb or goat. And not just any lamb or goat — the animal had to be male, 1 year old, and perfect looking. Every family or small community would bring their own.

These animals were offered to God as part of a special ritual in honor of the holiday. This was known as the "Korban Pesach," or "sacrifice of Passover."

Here's why: When the Israelites were still in Egypt, God told them to slaughter a lamb and spread the animal's blood on their doors. God was about to enact the final, and most serious, of the 10 plagues: death of the Egyptian firstborn sons. The blood on the door made it easy for the deadly force of God to know which houses had Israelites inside, so God did not accidentally kill any of them.

Now, back to the sacrifice at the Temple. When you slaughtered an animal as part of a sacrifice to God — Jews don't do this anymore, and haven't for a very long time — there were a lot of rules and prayers. First, priests sliced the animal's neck. Then, other priests would come by and collect the animal's blood in cups made of silver and gold. These cups were round on the bottom, so they couldn't be placed down on the ground. Then, the priests passed the cups of blood to other priests who were at the front of the Temple, or the altar, where they would sprinkle the blood in honor of God. During all this, the Jews would recite Psalms, or sacred songs of praise to God. You will recite some of the very same Psalms tonight under much less dramatic circumstances.

Eventually, the animal was roasted on skewers made of pomegranate wood and eaten as part of the Passover meal. If any lamb or goat was left over the next day, they weren't allowed to eat it, no matter how hungry they were. This was a sacred food that could only be eaten on a special day.

After the Temple got destroyed by the Romans, Jews stopped making the Korban Pesach. I love today's seders, which, by the way, are modeled on Roman banquets. But I would also love, even just once, to experience the intensity of Passover during the time of the Second Temple. Would you?

Ruby Namdar is a writer, scholar, and author of the award-winning novel "The Ruined House."

Before we can begin the seder, we light the candles and say the blessing below. If the seder falls on Shabbat, it is traditional to light the candles 18 minutes before sunset. This is also the only time we say a blessing after we perform a ritual.

LIGHT THE CANDLES.

בָּרוּךְ אַתָּה ה' אֱלֹהֵינוּ מֶלֶךְ הָעוֹלָם, אֲשֶׁר קִדְּשָׁנוּ בְּמִצְוֹתָיו וְצִוָּנוּ לְהַדְלִיק נֵר שֶׁל [שַׁבָּת וְ] שֶׁל יוֹם טוֹב.

Baruch atah adonai eloheinu melech ha'olam asher kid'shanu b'mitzvotav v'tzivanu l'hadlik ner shel [shabbat v'] yom tov.

Blessed are You, Adonai, Sovereign of the Universe, who makes us holy through Your commandments, and commands us to kindle the light of [Shabbat and] Yom Tov.

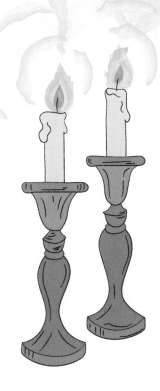

ORDER OF THE SEDER

The word seder means "order" in Hebrew. We call the Passover celebration and meal a seder because there's a particular order we follow. We've outlined it, step by step, below. Many people begin their seders by reading or singing these steps. You can do that now, if that's your family's tradition.

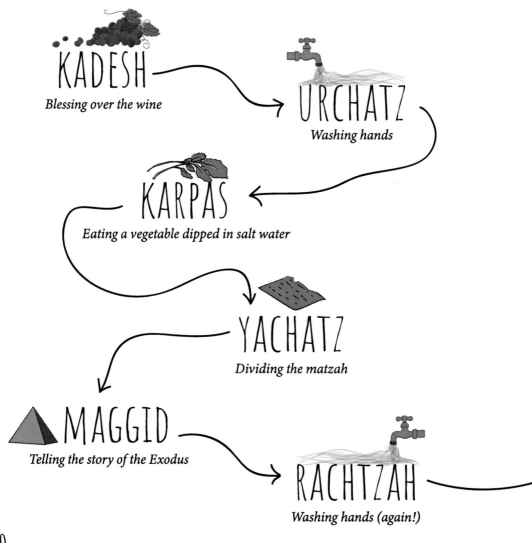

KADESH
Blessing over the wine

URCHATZ
Washing hands

KARPAS
Eating a vegetable dipped in salt water

YACHATZ
Dividing the matzah

MAGGID
Telling the story of the Exodus

RACHTZAH
Washing hands (again!)

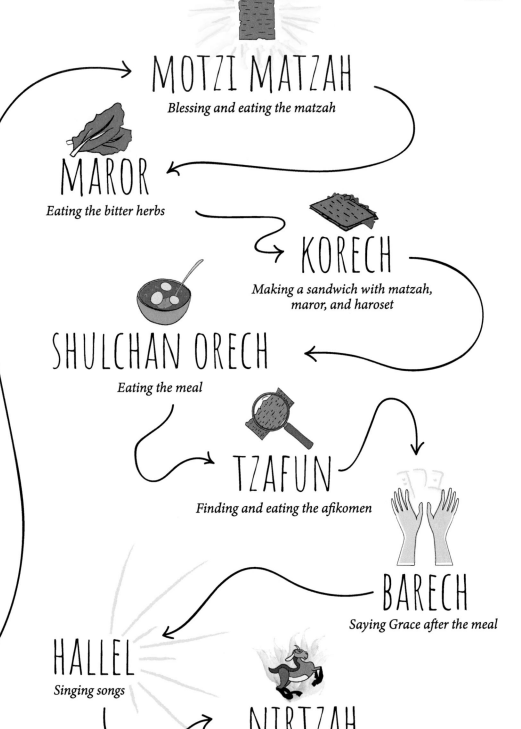

MOTZI MATZAH
Blessing and eating the matzah

MAROR
Eating the bitter herbs

KORECH
Making a sandwich with matzah, maror, and haroset

SHULCHAN ORECH
Eating the meal

TZAFUN
Finding and eating the afikomen

BARECH
Saying Grace after the meal

HALLEL
Singing songs

NIRTZAH
Conclusion (and more songs!)

KADESH
קַדֵּשׁ

In blessing the wine, we separate this moment and this meal from all other moments and meals.

First up, we raise our glasses and recite the following:

On Shabbat only:

וַיְהִי עֶרֶב וַיְהִי בֹקֶר יוֹם הַשִּׁשִּׁי. וַיְכֻלּוּ הַשָּׁמַיִם וְהָאָרֶץ וְכָל צְבָאָם.
וַיְכַל ה' בַּיּוֹם הַשְּׁבִיעִי מְלַאכְתּוֹ אֲשֶׁר עָשָׂה וַיִּשְׁבֹּת בַּיּוֹם הַשְּׁבִיעִי מִכָּל
מְלַאכְתּוֹ אֲשֶׁר עָשָׂה. וַיְבָרֶךְ ה' אֶת יוֹם הַשְּׁבִיעִי וַיְקַדֵּשׁ אוֹתוֹ כִּי בוֹ שָׁבַת
מִכָּל מְלַאכְתּוֹ אֲשֶׁר בָּרָא ה' לַעֲשׂוֹת.

Vay'hi erev bay'hi voker yom hashishi. Vay'chulu hashamayim v'haaretz v'chol tz'vaam. Vay'chal Elohim bayom hash'vi-i m'lachto asher asah. Vayishbot bayom hash'vi-i mikol m'lachto asher asah. Vay'varech Elohim et yom hash'vi-i vay'kadeish oto ki vo shavat mikol v'lachto asher bara Elohim laasot.

And it was evening, and it was morning, the sixth day. Now the whole universe — sky, earth, and all their array — was completed. God completed the work of creation on the seventh day and rested, for all the work was completed. Then God blessed the seventh day and called it holy, for God rested on that day, having completed the work of creation. *(Genesis 1:31-2:3)*

If it's not Shabbat, start here:

בָּרוּךְ אַתָּה ה' אֱלֹהֵינוּ מֶלֶךְ הָעוֹלָם בּוֹרֵא פְּרִי הַגָּפֶן.

Baruch atah Adonai, Eloheinu Melech haolam, borei pri hagafen.

Blessed are You, Adonai, Sovereign of the Universe, who creates the fruit of the vine.

בָּרוּךְ אַתָּה ה', אֱלֹהֵינוּ מֶלֶךְ הָעוֹלָם אֲשֶׁר בָּחַר בָּנוּ מִכָּל עָם וְרוֹמְמָנוּ מִכָּל לָשׁוֹן וְקִדְּשָׁנוּ בְּמִצְוֹתָיו. וַתִּתֶּן לָנוּ ה' אֱלֹהֵינוּ בְּאַהֲבָה (שַׁבָּתוֹת לִמְנוּחָה וּ) מוֹעֲדִים לְשִׂמְחָה, חַגִּים וּזְמַנִּים לְשָׂשׂוֹן, (אֶת יוֹם הַשַּׁבָּת הַזֶּה וְ) אֶת יוֹם חַג הַמַּצּוֹת הַזֶּה זְמַן חֵרוּתֵנוּ, (בְּאַהֲבָה) מִקְרָא קֹדֶשׁ זֵכֶר לִיצִיאַת מִצְרָיִם. כִּי בָנוּ בָחַרְתָּ וְאוֹתָנוּ קִדַּשְׁתָּ מִכָּל הָעַמִּים, (וְשַׁבָּת) וּמוֹעֲדֵי קָדְשֶׁךָ (בְּאַהֲבָה וּבְרָצוֹן) בְּשִׂמְחָה וּבְשָׂשׂוֹן הִנְחַלְתָּנוּ.

בָּרוּךְ אַתָּה ה', מְקַדֵּשׁ (הַשַּׁבָּת וְ) יִשְׂרָאֵל וְהַזְּמַנִּים.

Baruch atah Adonai, Eloheinu Melech haolam, asher bachar banu mikol am v'rom'manu mikol lashon v'kid'shanu b'mitzvotav. Vatiten lanu Adonai Eloheinu b'ahavah (Shabbatot lim'nuchah u) moadim l'simchah chagim uz'manim l'sason (et yom haShabbat hazeh v') et yom chag hamatzot hazeh z'man cheiruteinu (b'ahavah) mikra kodesh zeicher litziat Mitzrayim. Ki vanu vacharta v'otanu kidashta mikol haamim (v'Shabbat) umoadei kodsh'cha (b'ahavah uv'ratzon) b'simchah uv'sason hinchaltanu.

Baruch atah Adonai, m'kadeish (haShabbat v')Yisrael v'hazmanim.

Blessed are You, Adonai, sovereign of the universe, You have chosen us from all peoples, exalting us and sanctifying us with mitzvot. In Your love, Our God, You have given us (Sabbaths of rest,) feasts of gladness, and seasons of joy; (this Shabbat day and) this festival of matzot, season of our freedom, (in love,) a holy commemoration, a reminder of the Exodus from Egypt. God, You have chosen us from all peoples, consecrating us to your service, giving us (the Sabbath, a sign of your love and favor and) the Festivals, a time of gladness and joy.

Blessed are You, who sanctifies (Shabbat), our people Israel, and the Festivals.

Now, you can <u>drink</u> the grape juice or wine — and <u>lean back</u> and relax a little.

The seder includes four cups of wine, and this is the first one. Kids and adults may use grape juice instead.

(If it's Saturday evening and it's your tradition to do Havdalah, now is the time to do that. Otherwise, please continue below.)

On the first night of Passover, we say the Shehecheyanu blessing, a prayer that often marks a special "first." It could be a baby's first step or a child's first day of school, or the first night of a Jewish holiday. It is essentially a mindfulness prayer, in which we thank God for allowing us to reach this very moment. Many steps have led us to this occasion, and many more will likely follow, but the Shehecheyanu's focus is on gratitude for now.

בָּרוּךְ אַתָּה ה', אֱלֹהֵינוּ מֶלֶךְ הָעוֹלָם, שֶׁהֶחֱיָנוּ וְקִיְּמָנוּ וְהִגִּיעָנוּ לַזְּמַן הַזֶה.

*Baruch atah Adonai, Eloheinu Melech haolam,
shehecheyanu, v'kiyimanu, v'higiyanu la'z'man ha'zeh*

Blessed are You, Adonai, Sovereign of the Universe,
who has given us life, sustained us, and allowed us to
reach this day.

TOP SECRET

What's With All the Fours?

by Rabbi Shais Rishon, a.k.a. MaNishtana

The haggadah includes Four Questions, Four Cups of Wine, and Four Sons. What gives? Why so many fours?

One reason for all of these fours goes back to the Exodus story. At one point in the story, when Moses fears that things are getting worse for the Israelites, God assures Moses that things are about to get better.

God says:
V'hotzeti — "And I will bring you out."
V'hitzalti — "And I will deliver you."
V'ga'alti — "And I will redeem you."
V'lakachti — "And I will take you."

With these words, God vows to take the Israelite slaves out of Egypt, to deliver them to a new land, to help them become free people, and to be their God. The fours of the seder remind us of these promises. Each glass of wine or grape juice at the seder corresponds to one of these vows.

There are other significant fours in the Exodus story, too:

- *Pharoah made **four awful rules** for the Israelites: slavery, the private order to murder newborn Israelite boys during childbirth, the public order to drown newborn Israelite boys, and the demand that the Israelites collect their own straw for the bricks they built, which made their jobs even harder than before.*

- *The Israelites are said to have maintained **four distinct characteristics** while in bondage: they kept their language, they kept their names, they had no forbidden relationships with Egyptians, and they didn't tell on each other to their taskmasters.*

- *There are **four matriarchs of the Jewish people**: Sarah, Rebecca, Rachel, and Leah. The Israelite women in the Passover story honor their legacy by being kind and hopeful while they were slaves and during their escape from Egypt.*

- *Most importantly, **four Hebrew letters** make up God's name: yud, hay, vav, hay.*

That's a lot of fours and a lot to think about!

MaNishtana is a writer, playwright, speaker, novelist, and rabbi, whose work takes on prejudice and misconceptions about Orthodox Judaism, American Jewish racial identity, and African-American religious identity.

URCHATZ

Now, we wash our hands with water — no soap or blessing necessary. What if your hands are already clean? You still have to wash!

This commandment traces its roots back to the Torah's Book of Exodus, when Jews were very concerned about feeling clean and pure before a meal.

Today, some of us might also think about how the water makes our minds feel.

Some people wash their hands at the table with a bowl of water and a cup. Others wash their hands at the sink. Anyone feel renewed now? More ready to focus?

KARPAS

The good news: We get to eat. The bad news: It's only a vegetable, like celery or parsley, dipped in salt water or vinegar. The liquid represents the tears of the Israelite slaves in Egypt, who were sad and scared.

Remember what we said at the beginning of this haggadah about eating memories? Well, here goes.

But first, say this blessing:

בָּרוּךְ אַתָּה ה', אֱלֹהֵינוּ מֶלֶךְ הָעוֹלָם בּוֹרֵא פְּרִי הָאֲדָמָה.

Baruch atah adonai, eloheinu melech ha'olam, borei p'ri ha'adamah.

Blessed are you, Adonai, sovereign of the universe, who creates the fruit of the earth.

Now <u>dip</u> the vegetable in salt water and eat it.

Anyone feel like you were actually eating tears?

MEMORY LANE:

When Does Our Memory Turn On?

How come you don't remember being born? Or eating cake at your first birthday party? These are pretty important events in your life. Why didn't your brain store them? After all, you can easily remember the names of every kid in your class or the password for the iPad. Thing is, most people have trouble remembering things that happened to them before they were age 3, 4, or even 5.

Brain scientists aren't quite sure why that is. Some think that the brain doesn't create these kinds of memories (called episodic memories) early on; others think that those memories are created, but they can't be accessed later on. Either way, being unable to remember things that happened to us when we were very young is called "infantile amnesia."

But even if babies are not storing where-what-when memories, they are likely using a different kind of memory — one that allows most of them to learn to crawl and then to walk; to babble, and then to talk. They need to remember how all this is done so that they can do it again and build on those new skills.

Babies also have a kind of memory that allows them to feel things, and their bodies remember those feelings even if they can't yet turn them into stories. If a baby is bitten by a dog, say, she might be fearful of dogs for many years after. She might not know why exactly — but her body has stored that trauma.

Think about what baby Moses might have been feeling when his mother, Yocheved, left him on the banks of the river. Maybe he was feeling cold and hungry and eager for his mom to pick him up and nurse him. (We'll learn more about baby Moses when we tell the Passover story.)

Sources: Hadley Creighton Bergstrom, Memory Researcher, Vassar College; Amy Cohen, Child Psychiatrist

YACHATZ

Here, a grownup reaches under the covered pile of matzah and takes out the middle piece. Then that person breaks this piece in half.
The larger piece is the *afikomen*, which comes from a Greek word for "dessert" (literally, "that which comes after"), and it's the very last thing we're supposed to eat at the Passover seder.

At some point in the next hour or so, the *afikomen* may be wrapped in a napkin and hidden. There's probably a prize for the child who finds it. So keep your eyes on the *afikomen* — even if it's not what you had in mind for dessert. Don't worry, we're guessing there's probably some macaroons and jelly rings coming, too.

WHY? This night is all about telling our story to the next generation — to the children. The Talmudic Rabbis suggest various ways to keep kids interested and awake enough to stay involved. One of them, Rabbi Eliezer, says, "We snatch matzahs on the night of Passover in order that the children should not fall asleep." Over time this action, "snatching matzahs," got connected to the strange fact that we end the meal by eating matzah again — the *afikomen*. Thus "snatching the matzahs" came to mean "snatch them and hide them until the end," and turned into the most beloved way to keep children excited during this totally normal, not-at-all long dinner. (Yeah, right.)

MAGGID
HA LACHMA ANYA

Now someone at the table should <u>uncover</u> the matzah plate and raise up a piece of matzah. Say out loud:

הָא לַחְמָא עַנְיָא דִּי אֲכָלוּ אַבְהָתָנָא בְּאַרְעָא דְמִצְרָיִם. כָּל דִכְפִין
יֵיתֵי וְיֵיכֹל, כָּל דִצְרִיךְ יֵיתֵי וְיִפְסַח. הָשַׁתָּא הָכָא, לְשָׁנָה הַבָּאָה בְּאַרְעָא דְיִשְׂרָאֵל.
הָשַׁתָּא עַבְדֵי, לְשָׁנָה הַבָּאָה בְּנֵי חוֹרִין.

Ha lachma anya di achalu avhatana b'ara d'mitzrayim. Kol dichfin yeitei v'yeichol, kol ditzrich yeitei v'yifsach. Hashata hacha, l'shanah habaah b'ara d'yisrael. Hashata avdei, l'shanah habaah b'nei chorin.

This is a the bread of affliction that our ancestors ate in Egypt. Let all who are hungry come and eat. Let all who are in need come and share the Pesach meal. Now we are here, next year we will be in the land of Israel; this year we are slaves, next year we will be free.

WHY? A lot is going on here. First, we are reminding ourselves that we are not only supposed to learn about the Exodus — we actually feel like it is happening to us, too.

Second, we are remembering that there are still many people out there today who suffer like we once did in Egypt. The act of sharing this food, even if it is just a bland piece of matzah, helps us feel free. It's hard to share when you are a poor, hungry slave. Now, it's unlikely that a hungry person we don't know will hear us say this and then come to our house tonight to share our food. But perhaps sometime soon we can donate food or money or time to help feed hungry people.

Third, even those who aren't hungry may want to observe Passover, but have nowhere to go. Maybe they are new in town? Maybe their family lives far away? We must do our part to make sure they are welcomed into the community. Perhaps we can even make space for them at our own seder table.

Fourth, the seder is more than a meal — it's a journey. And if you've ever taken a trip, you know how our feelings tend to change throughout it. At the beginning, the matzah is the bread of affliction; at the end, it's the bread of freedom. At the beginning, the *haroset* represents the mortar used to make bricks as slaves; later on, it's the sweet taste of freedom. At the beginning of the seder, it's as if we are slaves; by the end, we are free!

THE 4 QUESTIONS
מה נשתנה?

It's time to recite the Four Questions. Usually it's the job of the youngest reader at the table, but some families have all the kids at the table do it together.

מַה נִּשְׁתַּנָּה הַלַּיְלָה הַזֶּה מִכָּל הַלֵּילוֹת?

Ma nishtanah halailah hazeh mikol haleilot?

Why is this night different from all other nights?

שֶׁבְּכָל הַלֵּילוֹת אָנוּ אוֹכְלִין חָמֵץ וּמַצָּה, הַלַּיְלָה הַזֶּה – כֻּלּוֹ מַצָּה.

Sheb'khol haleilot anu okhlin hametz umatzah; halailah hazeh, kuloh matzah.

On all other nights we eat leavened products and matzah.
Why on this night only matzah?

שֶׁבְּכָל הַלֵּילוֹת אָנוּ אוֹכְלִין שְׁאָר יְרָקוֹת – הַלַּיְלָה הַזֶּה כֻּלּוֹ מָרוֹר.

Sheb'khol haleilot anu okhlin sh'ar y'rakot; halailah hazeh, maror.

On all other nights we eat all vegetables.
Why on this night only bitter herbs?

שֶׁבְּכָל הַלֵּילוֹת אֵין אָנוּ מַטְבִּילִין אֲפִילוּ פַּעַם אֶחָת – הַלַּיְלָה הַזֶּה שְׁתֵּי פְעָמִים.

Sheb'khol haleilot ein anu matbilin afilu pa'am ehat; halailah hazeh, shtei f'amim.

On all other nights, we don't dip our food even once.
Why on this night do we dip twice?

שֶׁבְּכָל הַלֵּילוֹת אָנוּ אוֹכְלִין בֵּין יוֹשְׁבִין וּבֵין מְסֻבִּין – הַלַּיְלָה הַזֶּה כֻּלָּנוּ מְסֻבִּין.

Sheb'khol haleilot anu okhlin bein yoshvin uvein m'subin; halailah hazeh, kulanu m'subin.

On all other nights we eat sitting or reclining.
Why on this night do we all recline?

Want to know something funny? The seder doesn't usually directly answer these questions. Why do you think that is?

But in case you are wondering, here are the answers:

When the Israelites were leaving Egypt, they had to leave in a hurry. They prepared bread, but since there was no time to let the dough rise, they made a flatbread called *matzah* instead. Tonight, and for the next week, this is the bread we eat, too.

The bitter herbs remind us of the bitterness of slavery in the land of Egypt.

Dipping *karpas* in salt water or vinegar recalls the tears of slaves, and dipping bitter herbs into *haroset* suggests that the promise of something better sweetens even the most challenging times.

We recline because we are no longer slaves, and we have the luxury to relax sometimes.

21

WE WERE SLAVES IN EGYPT

AVADIM עֲבָדִים
HAYINU הָיִינוּ

Recite Together:

עֲבָדִים הָיִינוּ לְפַרְעֹה בְּמִצְרָיִם, וַיּוֹצִיאֵנוּ ה' אֱלֹהֵינוּ מִשָּׁם בְּיָד חֲזָקָה
וּבִזְרֹעַ נְטוּיָה. וְאִלּוּ לֹא הוֹצִיא הַקָּדוֹשׁ בָּרוּךְ הוּא אֶת אֲבוֹתֵינוּ מִמִּצְרָיִם,
הֲרֵי אָנוּ וּבָנֵינוּ וּבְנֵי בָנֵינוּ מְשֻׁעְבָּדִים הָיִינוּ לְפַרְעֹה בְּמִצְרָיִם.
וַאֲפִילוּ כֻּלָּנוּ חֲכָמִים כֻּלָּנוּ נְבוֹנִים כֻּלָּנוּ זְקֵנִים כֻּלָּנוּ יוֹדְעִים אֶת הַתּוֹרָה
מִצְוָה עָלֵינוּ לְסַפֵּר בִּיצִיאַת מִצְרָיִם. וְכָל הַמַּרְבֶּה לְסַפֵּר בִּיצִיאַת
מִצְרַיִם הֲרֵי זֶה מְשֻׁבָּח.

Avadim hayinu l'faroh b'mitzrayim. Vayotzieinu Adonai
Eloheinu misham, b'yad chazakah uvizroa n'tuyah, v'ilu lo hotzi
hakadosh baruch hu et avoteinu mimitzrayim, harei anu
uvaneinu uv'nei vaneinu, m'shubadim hayinu l'faroh
b'mitzrayim. Va'afilu kulanu chachamim, kulanu n'vonim,
kulanu z'keinim, kulanu yod'im et hatorah, mitzvah aleinu
l'sapeir biyitziat mitzrayim. V'chol hamarbeh l'sapeir biyitziat
mitzrayim, harei zeh m'shubach.

We were slaves to Pharaoh in the land of Egypt. And the Lord,
our God, took us out from there with a strong hand and an
outstretched forearm. And if the Holy One, blessed be God, had
not taken our ancestors from Egypt, behold we and our children
and our children's children would [all] be enslaved to Pharaoh
in Egypt. And even if we were all sages, all discerning, all elders,
all knowledgeable about the Torah, it would be a commandment
upon us to tell the story of the Exodus from Egypt. And anyone
who adds [and spends extra time] in telling the story of the
Exodus from Egypt, behold he is praiseworthy.

THE 4 BLESSINGS & THE 4 CHILDREN

We now say four blessings for the four Torah passages we are about to read in the story of the Four Children.

Recite together:

בָּרוּךְ הַמָּקוֹם, בָּרוּךְ הוּא, בָּרוּךְ שֶׁנָּתַן תּוֹרָה לְעַמּוֹ יִשְׂרָאֵל, בָּרוּךְ הוּא.

Baruch hamakom, baruch hu.
Baruch shenatan torah le'amo yisrael, baruch hu.

Blessed is the omnipresent one, blessed be God!
Blessed is God who gave the Torah to God people Israel,
blessed be God!

Tonight we learn a story about four children, and each of them has a different attitude towards the Passover story. One is wise, one is wicked, one is innocent, and one doesn't know how to ask.

The wise child asks her parents: "What is the meaning of the rituals, rules, and laws that the Eternal our God has commanded you?" *(Deuteronomy 6:20)* I want to understand all the rules surrounding our seder.

Her parents answer: We are so happy you asked! Wise children want to understand what is going on during the seder, so they can participate now and one day explain the seder to their children. One of the important rules is found in the Mishnah, a very old book of Jewish stories and laws. It says,

"We may not eat any dessert after we eat the Pesach sacrifice."
(Mishnah Pesachim 10:8) A long time ago, Jews used to honor
the holiday by sacrificing an animal. Today, we do it with this
seder and by eating matzah. This law is one of the last ones we
are supposed to learn about the seder. We are teaching it to
you because you are very curious and seem to want to know a
lot of the details and reasons behind why we do what we do.

The wicked child asks his parents: "What is this service to
you?" *(Exodus 12:26)*

His parents answer: That's actually not a nice thing to say, but
you might not even realize why. In your question, you asked
why Passover matters "to you." A better question would be,
"Why does this worship matter to us?" By saying "to you," you
act like you are not part of the Jewish people. Feeling
connected to one another is a very important part of Judaism.
The Torah says, "For the sake of what the LORD did for me
when I went out of Egypt." *(Exodus 13:8)* Notice how it says
"for me." When we read that line we are all supposed to
remember that God freed all of us.

By the way, we know the wise child also asked a question
ending in "you." Maybe we said her question was wise and
your question was wicked because we weren't paying enough
attention to you. Parents can be totally unfair. Or, maybe we
didn't pay attention to how the wise child ended her question,
because she seemed more interested in the seder, and her
question was very specific.

The innocent child asks her parents: "What is this?" *(Exodus
13:14)*

Her parents answer: We will start with a simple explanation.
"By the strength of hand the LORD brought us out of Egypt,

from the house of slaves." *(Exodus 13:14)* You don't seem to understand very much about the seder yet, and that is OK! You are doing the right thing by starting with simple questions. Eventually, when you learn more, you might ask more specific ones.

The child who doesn't know how to ask her parents anything.

Her parents observe her silence and realize they need to help her start the conversation. Maybe this is because she doesn't understand anything, or maybe it is because she thinks she already understands everything. But no matter how much you know, or think you know, there are always more questions to ask.

Her parents respond: The Torah says that parents are responsible for teaching our children about the Exodus. "And you shall explain to your children that day, 'It is because of what the LORD did for me when I went free from Egypt.'" *(Exodus 13:8)* We are supposed to do this with all children, no matter what kind of questions they ask, no matter if they ask them kindly or rudely or not at all. No matter how a child is acting or how he or she learns best, we must now find a way to teach them the lessons of Passover.

It's easy to read these questions and think, which child am I? Which one is my sibling, my parents, my relatives? A famous 20th-century rabbi named Menachem Mendel Schneerson once wrote that we should all think of ourselves as all four children. Each and every one of us has moments when we are wise, wicked, simple, and disconnected. The story of the Four Children reminds us to be aware that we all have all of these sides within us.

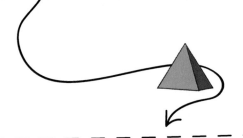

The Rebellion Began with Two Midwives
Rabbi Danya Ruttenberg

The Exodus story begins with midwives, and in a way it ends with midwives, too. Midwives, in case you don't know, are women who deliver babies. There are still midwives today — though now they can be women and men — and some of you may have been delivered by one.

Usually when we tell the story of Passover, we start with Moses. But actually the rebellion begins with two midwives, named Shifra and Puah. These women were instructed by Pharaoh to kill every Israelite boy during childbirth. But they bravely defied Pharaoh and didn't do it. Instead of killing the boys, they just lied to Pharaoh and said they didn't get there before the baby was born and couldn't do it. This was some pretty cool civil disobedience, right?

They even saved Moses' life. And since Moses would later lead the Israelites out of slavery, we have Shifra and Puah to thank for making our journey to freedom possible.

Some people think of the whole Exodus story as a birth story. The Israelites went through "a narrow place," like a birth canal. (The Hebrew word for Egypt, Mitzrayim, literally means, "narrow place.") The waters of the Red Sea parted like the waters that leave the womb before birth. Eventually, when they reached dry ground, Miriam, a prophet and Moses' sister, took a tambourine in her hand and she and the other women began to dance and sing. They were like midwives! The nation of Israel was being born, and there were the women helping bring this new people into a new world.

Rabbi Danya Ruttenberg is the author of "Nurture the Wow: Finding Spirituality in the Frustration, Boredom, Tears, Poop, Desperation, Wonder, and Radical Amazement of Parenting," and six other books. She has been named by Newsweek as one of 10 "rabbis to watch," and the Forward named her one of the top 50 most influential women rabbis.

V'HI SHE'AMDA

Now it's time to raise our glass and remember that the Jewish people's struggle for life and freedom didn't end when the Israelites left Egypt. Throughout history, others have tried to hurt us or get rid of us. But we are still here.

When we read this declaration, we honor the ways God has helped save us from destruction.

Recite together:

וְהִיא שֶׁעָמְדָה לַאֲבוֹתֵינוּ וְלָנוּ. שֶׁלֹּא אֶחָד בִּלְבָד עָמַד עָלֵינוּ לְכַלּוֹתֵנוּ,
אֶלָּא שֶׁבְּכָל דּוֹר וָדוֹר עוֹמְדִים עָלֵינוּ לְכַלּוֹתֵנוּ, וְהַקָּדוֹשׁ בָּרוּךְ הוּא מַצִּילֵנוּ מִיָּדָם.

*Vehi she'amda la'avotainu velanu. Shelo echad bilvad amad aleinu
lechaloteinu, ela sheb'chol dor vador omdim aleinu lechaloteinu,
v'hakadosh baruch hu matzilenu miyadam.*

And this (God and the Torah) is what kept our ancestors and
what keeps us surviving. For, not only one arose and tried to
destroy us, rather in every generation they try to destroy us,
but Adonai rescues us from their hands.

This time, we put our glasses down without taking a sip.

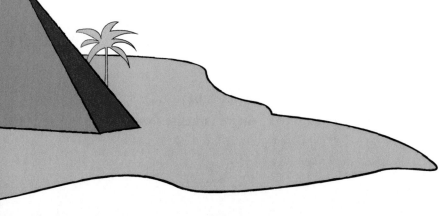

THE EXODUS STORY

Typically at Passover, we don't talk much about Moses because we are supposed to focus our attention on how God saved us. That said, here's a quick refresher of the Exodus story from the Torah. If you already know that story by heart, feel free to skip ahead to the 10 Plagues now.

The Exodus story begins with Joseph — an Israelite, the favorite son of the biblical patriarch Jacob, and a trusted aide of the Pharaoh. Joseph was a close friend of the Egyptians and even helped save the Egyptian people from famine, which is when people don't have enough food. But after Joseph grew old and died, the Pharaoh decided he didn't want to be nice to the Israelites anymore and made them slaves. That's pretty awful, but it gets even worse: Pharaoh didn't want there to be too many Israelites, in case they decided to fight back and demand their freedom. So he ordered all newborn Israelite boys to be tossed into the Nile River.

"No way!" said one young mother named Yocheved, who refused to drown her baby. Instead, she secretly left her newborn son in a basket at the edge of the river. Shortly after, Pharaoh's daughter discovered the boy and decided to raise him as her own child. She named him Moses. Then Yocheved, who was actually Moses' mom, became the baby's nurse.

And we cried out to the LORD, God of our parents, and the LORD heard our voice, and saw our abuse and our trouble and our oppression. (Deuteronomy 26:7)

Moses grew up to be a young man who cared about justice. So when he saw one of Pharaoh's deputies beat an Israelite slave, that made him SO MAD! In a fit of rage, Moses killed the Egyptian taskmaster. He then ran away, because staying behind would only lead to him getting punished by Egyptians. He left Egypt to become a shepherd and married Zipporah.

One day, while tending to his sheep, Moses saw a bush on fire. Strangely, however, it wasn't turning black or to ash or anything like that. Even stranger, the bush began to speak. It was God's voice, telling Moses to free the Israelite slaves. So back to Egypt Moses went, with God's message: "Let my people go." But Pharaoh, still cruel and selfish, said, "No."

God did not like Pharaoh's answer, and responded with the 10 plagues.

First, God turned the waters of Egypt into blood. Then, God brought frogs, lice, wild beasts, cattle disease, boils, hail, locusts that destroyed crops, and darkness that lasted three whole days. This was all terrible, but God's final plague was worst of all: the death of every firstborn in the land of Egypt.

10

PLAGUES

אֵלוּ עֶשֶׂר מַכּוֹת שֶׁהֵבִיא הַקָּדוֹשׁ בָּרוּךְ הוּא עַל־הַמִּצְרִים בְּמִצְרַיִם, וְאֵלוּ הֵן:

Eilu eser makot sheheivi hakadosh baruch hu al hamitzrim b'mitzrayim, v'eilu hein:

These are the plagues that the Holy Blessed One, brought upon Egypt:

It's time to recite the 10 plagues. As you say each one, dip one finger (many use their pinkies) into your wine or grape juice and touch it to your plate. Do not lick your fingers! By not tasting these drops, we are saying: We take no joy when other people suffer, even if the people suffering are our enemies. Their pain makes our joy a little less joyful and, in this case, our glasses a little less full.

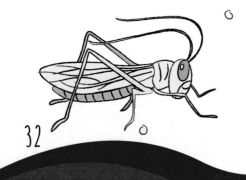

DAM דם
The Nile River turned to **_blood_**.

TZEFARDEAH צפרדע
Frogs were literally everywhere.

KINIM כינים
People and animals got itchy **_lice_**.

AROV ערוב
Dangerous **_wild beasts_** roamed around.

DEVER דבר
Animals, such as cows, horses, and sheep, **_got very sick_**.

SH'HIN שחין
People and animals broke out in painful **_boils_**.

BARAD ברד
Hail and lightning came from the sky.

ARBEH ארבה
Locusts destroyed the crops.

HOSHEKH חושך
Darkness covered the land for three straight days.

MACAT B'KHOROT מכת בכורות
All **_firstborn_** Egyptian sons were **_killed_**.

What's the Matter With Darkness?

You might notice that the plagues go from kind of bad to really bad to deadly. Lice isn't as scary as boils, and boils aren't as scary as death. Except, there's one plague that seems out of order: darkness. The dark can be scary, but it's also something that we are pretty used to — it comes at the end of each day, after all.

As Rabbi Jonathan Sacks explains, God had two targets in mind when ordering the plagues. One was the Egyptian people. The second were the Egyptians gods. God wanted to show everyone that God was more powerful than the sun, which the Egyptians worshipped as their most important god. Egyptians even believed that Pharaoh was the son of the sun god.

"And I will cross through the land of Egypt on this night, and I will strike down every firstborn in the land of Egypt from man to beast, and from all the gods of Egypt I will exact retributions." (Exodus 12:12)

Living in darkness wasn't just scary and bad for growing food and keeping people healthy; it also let Egyptians know that God was in charge. More importantly, God wanted to show disapproval for the way the Egyptians treat Pharaoh like a God and let him make some people slaves.

THE EXODUS STORY: PART 2

Now, back to our story. Pharaoh, worn down by the 10 plagues, finally agreed to free the Israelites. Unfortunately, the Israelites couldn't really believe him. In the past, Pharaoh would say one thing and then do another. The Israelites had no choice but to get out of there fast, before Pharaoh could change his mind. The preparation for their journey began right away, and they didn't have much time. Rather than wait for their bread to rise and bake, they grabbed the dough and let it bake in the sun as they ran away. (That's how we got flat, crunchy matzah instead of soft, fluffy bread.) And just as the Israelites predicted, Pharaoh changed his mind about letting his slaves go free. Moses was leading the Israelites out of Egypt when Pharaoh cut off their escape route and forced them to head right up to the banks of the Red Sea.

And the LORD brought us out from Egypt with a strong hand and an outstretched arm and with great terror and with signs and with portents. *(Deuteronomy 26:8)*

A dead end? Not for God! Moses raised his staff over the water, and then God parted the sea. The water split — and suddenly, briefly, there was a sandy path right in the middle. The Israelites escaped, and the Egyptigian soldiers chasing them were killed. This was the beginning of the Israelites' 40-year trek through the desert. The journey will be so hard that they will miss Egypt, but they keep going. They are on their way to the Promised Land.

DAYENU
(ABRIDGED)

Now it's time for a song to thank God for everything involved in bringing us out of slavery. Here, we say that even if God had only done one or two of those things, it would have been enough. But, as it turned out, God arranged for a great many more miracles to secure our freedom, and we are so grateful for that.

(The highlights are in bold.)

If God had only brought us out from Egypt,	*Ilu hotzianu mimitzrayim,*	אִלּוּ הוֹצִיאָנוּ מִמִּצְרַיִם
— Dayenu, it would have been enough!	*dayeinu!*	דַּיֵּנוּ
If God had split the sea for us,	*Ilu kara lanu et hayam,*	אִלּוּ קָרַע לָנוּ אֶת הַיָּם
and had not taken us through it on dry land	*v'lo he'eviranu b'tocho becharavah,*	וְלֹא הֶעֱבִירָנוּ בְּתוֹכוֹ בֶּחָרָבָה
— Dayenu, it would have been enough!	*dayeinu!*	דַּיֵּנוּ
If God had supplied our needs in the desert for 40 years,	*Ilu sipeik tzorkeinu bamidbar arba'im shana,*	אִלּוּ סִפֵּק צָרְכֵּנוּ בַּמִּדְבָּר אַרְבָּעִים שָׁנָה
and had not fed us the manna	*v'lo he'echilanu et haman,*	וְלֹא הָאֱכִילָנוּ אֶת הַמָּן
— Dayenu, it would have been enough!	*dayeinu!*	דַּיֵּנוּ
If God had fed us the manna,	*Ilu he'echilanu et haman,*	אִלּוּ הָאֱכִילָנוּ אֶת הַמָּן

and had not given us the Shabbat	*v'lo natan lanu et hashabbat,*	וְלֹא נָתַן לָנוּ אֶת הַשַּׁבָּת
— Dayenu, it would have been enough!	*dayeinu!*	דַּיֵּנוּ
If God had given us the Shabbat,	***Ilu natan lanu et hashabbat,***	**אִלּוּ נָתַן לָנוּ אֶת הַשַּׁבָּת**
and had not brought us before Mount Sinai	*v'lo keirvanu lifnei har sinai,*	וְלֹא קֵרְבָנוּ לִפְנֵי הַר סִינַי
— Dayenu, it would have been enough!	*dayeinu!*	**דַּיֵּנוּ**
If God had brought us before Mount Sinai,	*Ilu keirvanu lifnei har sinai,*	אִלּוּ קֵרְבָנוּ לִפְנֵי הַר סִינַי
and had not given us the Torah	*v'lo natan lanu et hatorah,*	וְלֹא נָתַן לָנוּ אֶת הַתּוֹרָה
— Dayenu, it would have been enough!	*dayeinu!*	דַּיֵּנוּ
If God had given us the Torah,	***Ilu natan lanu et hatorah,***	**אִלּוּ נָתַן לָנוּ אֶת הַתּוֹרָה**
and had not brought us into the land of Israel	*v'lo hichnisanu l'eretz yisra'eil,*	וְלֹא הִכְנִיסָנוּ לָאָרֶץ יִשְׂרָאֵל
— Dayenu, it would have been enough!	*dayeinu!*	**דַּיֵּנוּ**
If God had brought us into the land of Israel,	*Ilu hichnisanu l'eretz yisra'eil,*	אִלּוּ הִכְנִיסָנוּ לָאָרֶץ יִשְׂרָאֵל
and not built for us the Holy Temple	*v'lo vanah lanu et beit hamikdash,*	וְלֹא בָּנָה לָנוּ אֶת בֵּית הַמִּקְדָּשׁ
— Dayenu, it would have been enough!	*dayeinu!*	דַּיֵּנוּ

37

RABBAN GAMLIEL
AND HIS THREE THINGS

Rabban Gamliel was a very wise Jewish teacher who lived around 2,000 years ago. He used to say that everyone needs to discuss three things on Passover: the Passover sacrifice, matzah, and *maror*. If we don't, he believed, we haven't fulfilled our obligation to observe the holiday. When we talk about these three things, it allows us to feel as though the Exodus is happening to us.

Recite Together:

בְּכָל דּוֹר וָדוֹר חַיָּבִים אָנוּ לִרְאוֹת אֶת עַצְמֵנוּ כְּאִלּוּ
יָצְאנוּ מִמִּצְרַיִם

*B'khol dor vador khayavim anu lir'ot et
atzmeynu k'ilu yatzanu mimitzrayim.*

In every generation, it is our duty to consider
ourselves as if we had come forth from Egypt.

HALLEL

Now, we are going to sing a song of praise, thanking God for taking us out of Egypt and leading us to a better place. Hallel literally means "praise."

הַלְלוּיָהּ
הַלְלוּ עַבְדֵי ה', הַלְלוּ אֶת־שֵׁם ה'.
יְהִי שֵׁם ה' מְבֹרָךְ מֵעַתָּה וְעַד עוֹלָם.
מִמִּזְרַח שֶׁמֶשׁ עַד מְבוֹאוֹ מְהֻלָּל שֵׁם ה'. רָם עַל־כָּל־גּוֹיִם ה', עַל הַשָּׁמַיִם כְּבוֹדוֹ.
מִי כַּייָ אֱלֹהֵינוּ הַמַּגְבִּיהִי לָשָׁבֶת, הַמַּשְׁפִּילִי לִרְאוֹת בַּשָּׁמַיִם וּבָאָרֶץ?
מְקִימִי מֵעָפָר דָּל, מֵאַשְׁפֹּת יָרִים אֶבְיוֹן, לְהוֹשִׁיבִי עִם־נְדִיבִים, עִם נְדִיבֵי עַמּוֹ.
מוֹשִׁיבִי עֲקֶרֶת הַבַּיִת, אֵם הַבָּנִים שְׂמֵחָה.
הַלְלוּיָהּ.

Halleluyah
hal'lu avdei adonai, hal'lu et sheim adonai.
Y'hi sheim Adonai m'vorach mei'atah v'ad olam.
Mimizrach shemesh ad m'vo'o m'hulal sheim adonai. Ram al kol
goyim adonai, al hashamayim k'vodo.
Mi k'adonai eloheinu hamagbihi lashavet, hamashpili lirot
bashamayim uva'aretz?
M'kimi mei'afar dal, mei'ashpot yarim evyon, l'hoshivi im nidivim,
im nidivei amo.
Moshivi akeret habayit, eim habanim s'meichah.
Halleluyah.

Hallelujah,
Praise, O servants of the LORD, praise the LORD's name.
May the Lord's name be blessed now and forevermore. …
God raises the poor from the dust, from the dunheap lifts the needy,
to seat him among princes, among the princes of his people.
God seats the barren woman in her home a happy mother of sons.
Hallelujah.
(Psalm 113)

It Was Hard For Moses to Speak
by Rabbi Ruti Regan

Did you know that Moses had a disability? He had trouble speaking and his voice was hard to understand. Some people believe this was a stutter. Others believe his disability was something like cerebral palsy that affected other parts of his body, too.

When God told Moses that it was his job to lead the people out of Egypt, Moses resisted. "Why would Pharaoh or the Israelites believe me?" Moses wondered. So God gave Moses the power to turn his walking stick into a snake and to perform other miracles. Now Moses would be able to prove that he was telling the truth.

Still, Pharaoh was a very powerful king, and Moses worried that Pharaoh would not listen to someone who had trouble speaking. God told Moses that God makes everyone just the way they are on purpose "nonspeaking or deaf, seeing or blind." (Exodus 4:11) Even so, Moses thought that God must be making a mistake, and said, "Please, Lord, send someone else instead."

God insisted Moses was the right leader and that being the leader didn't mean he had to do everything himself. Instead, his brother, Aaron, could help him. When Moses didn't think his voice would work, he could tell Aaron what to say instead. When Moses didn't have the strength to hold up something, he could tell Aaron what to do instead.

In choosing Moses, God shows us that people with disabilities who need help can be leaders, that their helpers need to listen to the people they are helping, and that a person's voice doesn't have to work perfectly for them to have something important to say.

Rabbi Ruti Regan is a feminist rabbi, a disabled disability activist, an inclusive Jewish educator, and a blogger at realsocialskills.org.

SECOND CUP OF WINE

בָּרוּךְ אַתָּה ה', אֱלֹהֵינוּ מֶלֶךְ הָעוֹלָם בּוֹרֵא פְּרִי הַגָּפֶן.

Baruch ata adonai, eloheinu melech ha'olam, borei pri hagafen.

Blessed are You, Adonai, Sovereign of the Universe, who creates the fruit of the vine.

If you got thirsty with all of that storytelling, good news: You get to drink what's in your cup now. If you're at the edge of your seat (it's a pretty exciting story!), you can lean back and relax.

RACHTZAH

It's time to wash your hands again. This time there's a blessing — and that means that soon it's time to eat.

WHY? You may be wondering, didn't we just wash our hands? Usually, washing our hands before a meal means we're about to eat. But not on Passover. At the seder, we actually start the meal twice. The first time is really just a pretend beginning.

"The first time we wash it seems like a normal holiday meal: we make *kiddush*, we wash, but now we notice something is wrong," observed a contemporary rabbi named Rona Shapiro. "We don't say a blessing. We break bread, but we don't eat it."

As Rabbi Shapiro explains: On Passover, before we're ready to dig in, we must first tell the story of the Exodus and taste the unusual foods on the seder plate to understand better how they connect to that story.

Then, we wash our hands again and there's a blessing. We bless the matzah and we eat it. The meal begins for a second time, and this time it's for real.

You can either get up and go to the sink and use a cup there, or pass a bowl of water and a pitcher around the table. As you are <u>washing</u> your hands, this is the blessing <u>you say</u>:

בָּרוּךְ אַתָּה ה', אֱלֹהֵינוּ מֶלֶךְ הָעוֹלָם, אֲשֶׁר קִדְּשָׁנוּ בְּמִצְוֹתָיו וְצִוָּנוּ עַל נְטִילַת יָדָיִם.

Baruch ata adonai, eloheinu melech ha'olam, asher kid'shanu b'mitzvotav v'tzivanu al n'tilat yadayim.

Blessed are You, Adonai, Sovereign of the Universe, who makes us holy through Your commandments, and commands us regarding the washing of the hands.

It is customary not to speak between the time you wash your hands and the time you break bread or matzah (after someone makes a blessing). But feel free to hum or sing quietly.

MOTZI

It's time for the blessing over the bread, but because it's Passover we'll be eating matzah. It's the same prayer, though, and you may know it because it's one of the very first prayers many Jewish children learn. Then, there's a second blessing that mentions the matzah God commanded us to eat on Passover. **Recite them now.**

בָּרוּךְ אַתָּה ה', אֱלֹהֵינוּ מֶלֶךְ הָעוֹלָם הַמּוֹצִיא לֶחֶם מִן הָאָרֶץ.

Baruch ata adonai, eloheinu melech ha'olam hamotzi lechem min haaretz.

Blessed are You, Adonai, Sovereign of the Universe, who brings forth bread from the ground.

בָּרוּךְ אַתָּה ה', אֱלֹהֵינוּ מֶלֶךְ הָעוֹלָם, אֲשֶׁר קִדְּשָׁנוּ בְּמִצְוֹתָיו וְצִוָּנוּ עַל אֲכִילַת מַצָּה.

Baruch ata adonai, eloheinu melech ha'olam, asher kidshanu b'mitzvotav v'tzivanu al achilat matzah.

Blessed are You, Adonai, Sovereign of the Universe, who makes us holy through Your commandments, and commands us to eat matzah.

MATZAH

It's crunch time! Now you <u>eat</u> some matzah. Take a bite, or 10, and you can <u>lean back</u> or even slouch if you want.

As we already learned, the Israelites made matzah when preparing food for their journey out of Egypt. Eating this food doesn't just remind us of their harrowing escape — it also makes us feel like we are the ones leaving Egypt all these years later.

WHY? Would anyone here describe matzah as a fancy, indulgent food? Does it bear any resemblance to, say, a bagel, or warm challah fresh out of the oven? Nope. It is dry, it is brittle, and it kind of tastes like… nothing. Eating matzah is a humbling experience. The Torah calls it *lechem oni*, which means "bread of affliction," or, in other words, "poor man's bread." Matzah reminds us of what it is like to live through hard times, when we don't get to eat special things.

43

MEMORY LANE:

Food Memories Are Powerful for Good Reason

By John S. Allen

Many years ago, when I was a small child, I got separated from my parents at a store. The sales clerks who cared for me until my parents found me gave me popcorn in a little white box. Luckily, I still like popcorn. But to this day, popcorn makes me think of being lost in that store — bringing up negative memories of being lost and scared, and positive ones because, eventually, my parents found me and I was "rescued."

Why are food memories so powerful? It has to do with how our insides work. You see, the chemical messengers in our bodies (called hormones) that are important for controlling our appetite and digesting food have strong connections to the part of the brain (called the hippocampus) that we need to form new memories. When we eat, our ability to remember is especially strong. For animals that have to move around to find their meals, it's really important for them to remember where they have found food in the past. So the connection between taste and memory makes perfect sense.

For us humans, meals like this Passover seder are not just food feasts, they're memory feasts, too. Being with friends and family, connecting to our faith and history, and eating foods that remind us of our history and community make for a more memorable meal than your average lunchbox fare.

Oh, and the hippocampus has strong connections to another part of the brain that helps control emotions. This means emotional memories about food are likely to stay with us for a very long time.

John S. Allen is anthropologist and writer with a focus on the evolution of the human brain and behavior. He is the author of several books, including "The Omnivorous Mind: Our Evolving Relationship With Food."

MAROR

The Israelites — and everyone else who has ever been forced to work without any choice and not get paid for it — suffered a lot. There is no sugarcoating how bad slavery was, which is why, when we think about slavery, we don't eat sweet foods. Instead, we eat bitter foods, which remind us of the bitterness of slavery. A tiny bit of their pain is ours now to take in. And speaking of tiny, you only need a really tiny bit of these herbs to experience the bitterness. **Here's the blessing:**

בָּרוּךְ אַתָּה ה', אֱלֹהֵינוּ מֶלֶךְ הָעוֹלָם, אֲשֶׁר קִדְּשָׁנוּ בְּמִצְוֹתָיו וְצִוָּנוּ עַל אֲכִילַת מָרוֹר.

Baruch ata adonai, eloheinu melech ha'olam asher kid'shanu b'mitzvotav v'tzivanu al achilat maror.

Blessed are You, Adonai, Sovereign of the Universe, who makes us holy through Your commandments, and commands us to eat maror.

Now <u>sit up</u> (no leaning back here), and <u>take a tiny bite</u>. How bitter was it? Going back for more?

KORECH

A long time ago, there was a great rabbi named Hillel. He thought being kind was the most important thing, even more important than studying. He once said: "That which is hateful to you, do not do to others. That is the whole Torah; the rest is commentary; go and learn."

Rabbi Hillel had a special Passover tradition. Every seder, he would make a sandwich out of matzah, a slice of the sacrificial lamb, and a bitter herb. Since Jews don't sacrifice lambs anymore, today we make the sandwich with matzah, *haroset*, and a bitter herb. Now we are all going to do the same.

זֵכֶר לְמִקְדָּשׁ כְּהַלֵּל. כֵּן עָשָׂה הַלֵּל בִּזְמַן שֶׁבֵּית הַמִּקְדָּשׁ הָיָה קַיָּם: הָיָה כּוֹרֵךְ מַצָּה וּמָרוֹר וְאוֹכֵל בְּיַחַד, לְקַיֵּם מַה שֶׁנֶּאֱמַר: עַל מַצּוֹת וּמְרוֹרִים יֹאכְלֻהוּ.

Zeicher l'mikdash k'Hileil. Kein asah Hileil bizman shebeit hamikdash hayah kayam.
Hayah koreich pesach, matzah, u-maror v'ocheil b'yachad. L'kayeim mah shene-emar. "Al matzaht um'rorim yochlu-hu."

In memory of the Temple according to Hillel. This is what Hillel would do when the Temple existed: He would wrap the matzah and maror and eat them together, in order to fulfill what is stated: "You should eat it upon matzot and marorim." *(Numbers 9:11)*

WHY? It's kind of weird eating something bitter and sweet together at once, right? But eating this sandwich helps us feel all the complicated feelings of Passover at the same time.

The bitter herbs remind us of the bitterness of slavery in Egypt and of our sad memories. The matzah and *haroset* remind us of the fact we are free and of our sweet memories. We are not supposed to forget either one. And believe it or not, the sandwich is actually pretty tasty.

Give it a try! Take a bite of your sandwich.

SHULCHAN ORECH

And now, the moment we've all been waiting for: It's time to EAT!!

As you eat a delicious dinner, you can talk about whatever you like. Dinosaurs? Baseball? Dinosaurs playing baseball? Or try asking everyone around the table to share a sweet memory and then a bitter one. Or you can think ahead to a year from now: What do you think you will remember from tonight?

AFTER THE MEAL, IT'S TIME TO LOOK FOR THE AFIKOMEN!

Bonus idea: Kids, why don't you go hide an afikomen for your parents to find?

LET'S

EAT!

TZAFUN

Have you found the *afikomen* yet?

Whoever finds it must now return it to the seder's leader, or leaders, in exchange for a little something. It could be money, or it could be a toy! Maybe it's candy, or maybe it's more parsley! (Though we sure hope not.)

There are some rules, however: The *afikomen* must be the last thing you eat tonight. So make sure you have had your last bite of cake or cookies or fruit and only have room left for a teeny, tiny piece of matzah. (If your *afikomen* has turned to dust, it's OK to substitute another piece of matzah.)

WHY? Yes, it's weird to eat matzah for dessert. Matzah doesn't taste sweet — but the freedom it represents is! Remember how when we started, we said it was the bread of slavery? Now it is the taste of freedom! Look around your messy table. Pay attention to your friends and family, your full bellies, and the warm light glowing overhead. It's nice, isn't it?

Tzafun means "hidden." When we eat this last piece of matzah, we are supposed to be reconnecting with the parts of ourselves that we felt like we had to hide when we were slaves. Do you feel free?

BARECH

We ate, it was great, and now it's time to say the blessing after the meal. **First, go ahead and <u>pour</u> another glass of wine or grape juice; you'll need it soon.**

Some families do this with the traditional Birkat HaMazon. You can find this whole prayer — it's a long one — in a separate little prayer book sometimes known as a "bencher" (it comes from the Yiddish word "bentshn," meaning "to bless").

But there is a tradition that tells us that if you are being chased by robbers or wild animals, there's a shorter version you could use. Sometimes, a loud, long family meal might feel like a wild animal encounter, so feel free to use this one here:

בְּרִיךְ רַחֲמָנָא
מַלְכָּא דְּעָלְמָא
מָרֵיה דְּהַאי פִּתָּא

Brich rahamana
Malka d'alma
Ma'arey d'hai pita

Blessed is the merciful one,
ruler of the world,
creator of this bread.

Others might just take a minute to feel the love, or simply say, "Thanks!" out loud. On the count of three: 1… 2… 3… *Thaaaaaaanks!*

THE THIRD CUP
+ ELIJAH'S CUP

Even though we are done eating, we still have two more cups of wine or grape juice to drink, plus another cup that we do something a little unusual with.

בָּרוּךְ אַתָּה ה', אֱלֹהֵינוּ מֶלֶךְ הָעוֹלָם בּוֹרֵא פְּרִי הַגָּפֶן.

Baruch atah Adonai, Eloheinu Melech haolam, borei pri hagafen.

Blessed are You, Adonai, Sovereign of the Universe, who creates the fruit of the vine.

Drink up. We're almost there.

Now, we are going to pour a glass of wine and open our front door for a prophet named Elijah. Will he drink the wine? Kids, pay close attention to the cup and see if any of what's inside disappears.

WHY? The Prophet Elijah (a.k.a. Eliyahu Hanavi) ascended to Heaven while still alive, and so the rabbis saw him as a unique figure who was able to travel freely between the Heaven and Earth. Jews consider Elijah to be a messenger of God, which means God tells Elijah what God is thinking or feeling, and Elijah shares with us what God said. According to a later prophet, Elijah will also be the one to bring the message that redemption, a future time of peace on earth, is coming. That's why we call on Elijah at moments when we focus on our hopes for the future, like the end of Shabbat and the birth of a new baby. On Passover, we go a step further — we invite Elijah, and what he represents, into our homes: the hope for a better, brighter future.

Now, let's <u>call out</u> to Elijah by reciting or singing "Eliyahu Hanavi."

אֵלִיָּהוּ הַנָּבִיא אֵלִיָּהוּ הַתִּשְׁבִּי אֵלִיָּהוּ הַגִּלְעָדִי בִּמְהֵרָה בְיָמֵינוּ יָבוֹא
אֵלֵינוּ עִם מָשִׁיחַ בֶּן דָּוִד.

Eliyahu hanavi, Eliyahu hatishbi, Eliyahu hagiladi.
Bimheirah b'yameinu, yavo eileinu, im Mashiach ben David.

May Elijah the prophet, Elijah the Tishbite, Elijah of Gilead,
quickly in our day come to us heralding redemption.

Now recite together:

שְׁפֹךְ חֲמָתְךָ אֶל־הַגּוֹיִם אֲשֶׁר לֹא יְדָעוּךָ
וְעַל־מַמְלָכוֹת אֲשֶׁר בְּשִׁמְךָ לֹא קָרָאוּ.
כִּי אָכַל אֶת־יַעֲקֹב וְאֶת־נָוֵהוּ הֵשַׁמּוּ.
שְׁפָךְ־עֲלֵיהֶם זַעְמֶךָ וַחֲרוֹן אַפְּךָ יַשִּׂיגֵם.
תִּרְדֹּף בְּאַף וְתַשְׁמִידֵם מִתַּחַת שְׁמֵי ה'.

Shfoch chamatcha el hagoyim asher lo y'da'ucha
v'al mamlachot asher b'shimcha lo kara'u.
Ki achal et Ya'akov v'et naveihu heishamu.
Shfoch Aleihem zamech vacharon apcha yasigaim.
Tirdof b'af v'tashmidaim mitachat shmay Adonai.

Pour out your wrath upon the nations that did not know You
and upon the kingdoms that did not call upon Your Name!
Since they have consumed Ya'akov and laid waste his
habitation *(Psalms 79:6-7)*. Pour out Your fury upon them
and the fierceness of Your anger shall reach them *(Psalms
69:25)*! You shall pursue them with anger and eradicate them
from under the skies of the Lord *(Lamentations 3:66)*.

WHY? Anyone wondering what this burst of anger is doing near the
end of the seder? So much of tonight has been about remembering
our journey out of Egypt and celebrating our new freedom. And now,
we are told we're supposed to feel really mad at those who hurt us —
so mad, in fact, that we want to punish them for what they did.

We say this to remember the anger God and the Israelites must have
felt about what Pharaoh did. It's common to feel angry when
someone has treated us unfairly or caused us pain. Anger is a
powerful force, one that can drive us to do good things, like make
changes in our lives and our world. But it can also make us lose our
good judgment and hurt other people. When we voice our anger, it
gives us a chance to reflect upon it. We get a chance to figure out what
or whom we are really mad at, whether they deserve our anger, and if
we can channel it for good.

HALLEL

Anyone remember what Hallel means?

That's right, "praise!" And it's time to do it again.

Yes, we are all very tired and full. But this is our last chance to show appreciation for our freedom and our community. So get up and take a stretch if you need to, then let's sit our tushes right back down and say thank you. Leave it all on the field — or at the seder table. Sing loudly! Wave your hands around. Make such a ruckus that your neighbors come over to make sure you are OK!

Traditional Jews recite Psalms 115-118 right now. Here is our abridged version:

Psalm 116:5-9
Gracious the LORD and just,
and our God shows mercy.
The LORD protects the simple.
I plunged down, but me God did rescue.
Return, my being, to your calm,
for the LORD has requited you.
For You freed me from death,
my eyes from tears, my foot from slipping.
I shall walk before the LORD In the lands of the living.

Psalm 117
Praise the LORD, all nations;
Extol God, all peoples.
For God's kindness overwhelms us,
and the LORD'S steadfast truth is forever.
Hallelujah.

MEMORY LANE:

How Does Your Brain Make a Memory?

Memories are encoded in our brains, with the help of electricity. Here's how it works:

First, we experience something like eating matzah ball soup. We remember the taste of the soup, the way it looked, what we were talking about while we ate it, and the fact that our little sister spilled some of her soup on our lap. Ouch!

These are sensory experiences, and they travel up into our brains where they are transferred into electrical signals and sent to a place in the brain called the cerebral cortex.

The cerebral cortex sends those electrical signals along to another part of the brain where the memory is encoded, or formed. The tastes, the conversation, the hot soup on the lap — it all gets put together as a single memory.

Then something crazy happens. The memory is then sent back to the cerebral cortex, where it is actually broken back up into different experiences and stored away in different parts of the brain. The taste goes to the part of the brain that remembers tastes, and the conversation goes to the part of the brain that remembers conversations, and the hot soup on the lap goes to the place that remembers how our bodies feel.

Then another crazy thing happens. When you recall this memory, the brain pulls it all back together and ... ta-da! All the parts of the memory are back together again.

Source: Nanthia Suthana, Neuroscientist

THE FOURTH CUP

Had enough wine or grape juice? Some rabbis say that the smallest amount that counts as a cup is 1.7 ounces — that's much less than the 5 ounces that's in a typical glass of red wine.

It's time for the blessing over the wine, one last time.

בָּרוּךְ אַתָּה ה', אֱלֹהֵינוּ מֶלֶךְ הָעוֹלָם בּוֹרֵא פְּרִי הַגָּפֶן.

Baruch atah Adonai, Eloheinu Melech haolam, borei pri hagafen.

Blessed are You, Adonai, Sovereign of the Universe, who creates the fruit of the vine.

Sit back and relax, and take a sip. Or a gulp.

NIRTZAH

We've reached the end. But it isn't over yet.

Wait, what?

Some believe that even though we will all leave the table and go to sleep soon, the seder is never really done. Every day, we should think of ourselves as leaving Egypt. We need to keep on fighting for freedom for others. We need to keep on thinking about ways we can feel free. We need to keep on trying to feel connected to each other, our families, our communities, and with God. And to do this, we need to make, hold, and share our memories, person to person, generation to generation. Memories bind us to each other and the past and give us the wisdom and the strength to embrace what's ahead.

It is customary for the last words we recite at this table to be: Next year in Jerusalem. And that's not necessarily because that's where our seder will be next year, though it could be. We might also be thinking about the idea of Jerusalem. The name "Jerusalem" means the "city of peace and wholeness" — wouldn't it be wonderful to live in a time and place where everything felt peaceful and whole?

Our tradition tells us that the Hebrew word Jerusalem, *Yerushalayim*, ends with a plural "*im*" because there are two Jerusalems. There is the ideal, a city of peace and wholeness that we are supposed to build, and there is the real Jerusalem, a beautiful city of gold that is also a really hard and complicated place. That's true of our lives, too. There's what we want — what we're working toward — and there's the reality of our day-to-day, which can be more challenging than we'd like. Our job is to see ourselves in both places, and as we do to try to bring them a little closer together.

So whether or not we think next year will bring us to Israel, "Next year in Jerusalem" is a declaration of hope — hope that the Jewish people's ancient and ongoing story (our story!) will lead to happy and holy places in the next year and beyond.

Now, everyone, together:

לְשָׁנָה הַבָּאָה בִּירוּשָׁלָיִם.

L'Shana Haba'ah B'Yerushalayim.

NEXT YEAR IN JERUSALEM.

Were the Israelites really free?

Rabbi Sari Laufer

Whew! We made it! Do you feel different? Do you feel free?

For the Israelites, it must have been so exciting to be free. The Torah says that after crossing the Red Sea, they sang and danced. But we also know that after all the celebrating, they started complaining. They were tired and hungry, and probably scared. They didn't know where they were going or how they would get there.

The Torah also says that, at this point, God told the Israelites where to go, what to do, what to eat, and even sometimes how to eat.

Wait a minute. Didn't we just say that they were free? The whole point of the story was that they no longer had to listen to Pharaoh telling them what to do. But now that they had left Egypt, God was telling them what to do. So were the Israelites really free?

Most of us learn that God told Moses to tell Pharoah to "let my people go." But that wasn't all God asked. What God actually said was: "Tell Pharaoh to let my people go so that they may serve Me." That's right, God wanted Pharoah to let the Israelites go, so that they may serve God — or follow God's rules.

This is kind of confusing, right? Some people might not see following God's rules as freedom. They think freedom means being able to do whatever you want, whenever you want. But that's not what we get.

So, now we are free from Egypt. And what does this freedom look like? We are free to celebrate our holidays and sing our songs and pray our prayers. We are free to think about and ask questions and argue about the rules. We are free to rely on our traditions and rituals to guide us on our own journey. We are free to make choices, but that doesn't mean we are free to do whatever we want all the time.

And for me, that feels like just the right amount of freedom. How about you?

Rabbi Sari Laufer is a rabbi at Stephen Wise Temple in Los Angeles, where she is the Director of Congregational Engagement. She lives in L.A. with her husband and children.

CHAD GADYA

"Chad gadya" means "one little goat" in Aramaic, an ancient language with many similarities to Hebrew. It was also the language many Jews spoke when most of the seder rituals were created.

One little goat, one little goat,
that Father bought for two zuzim,
Chad gadya, chad gadya.

Chad gadya, chad gadya,
dizabin aba bitrei zuzei,
chad gadya, chad gadya.

Then came a cat
and ate the goat,
that Father bought for two zuzim,
Chad gadya, chad gadya.

Va'ata shunra,
ve'achla legadya
dizabin aba bitrei zuzei,
chad gadya, chad gadya.

Then came a dog
and bit the cat,
that ate the goat,
that Father bought for two zuzim,
Chad gadya, chad gadya.

Va'ata chalba,
venashach leshunra
de'achla legadya
dizabin aba bitrei zuzei,
chad gadya, chad gadya.

Then came a stick
and beat the dog,
that bit the cat,
that ate the goat,
that Father bought for two zuzim,
Chad gadya, chad gadya.

Va'ata chutra,
vehikah lechalba,
denashach leshunra
de'achla legadya
dizabin aba bitrei zuzei,
chad gadya, chad gadya.

Then came fire
and burnt the stick,
that beat the dog,
that bit the cat,
that ate the goat,
that Father bought for two zuzim,
Chad gadya, chad gadya.

Then came water
and quenched the fire,
that burnt the stick,
that beat the dog,
that bit the cat,
that ate the goat,
that Father bought for two zuzim,
Chad gadya, chad gadya.

Then came the ox
and drank the water,
that quenched the fire,
that burnt the stick,
that beat the dog,
that bit the cat,
that ate the goat,
that Father bought for two zuzim,
Chad gadya, chad gadya.

Then came the slaughterer
and slaughtered the ox,
that drank the water,
that quenched the fire,
that burnt the stick,
that beat the dog,
that bit the cat,
that ate the goat,
that Father bought for two zuzim,
Chad gadya, chad gadya.

Va'ata nura,
vesaraf lechutra,
dehikah lechalba,
denashach leshunra
de'achla legadya
dizabin aba bitrei zuzei,
chad gadya, chad gadya.

Va'ata maya,
vekavah lenura,
desaraf lechutra,
dehikah lechalba,
denashach leshunra
de'achla legadya
dizabin aba bitrei zuzei,
chad gadya, chad gadya.

Va'ata tora,
veshatah lemaya,
dekavah lenura,
desaraf lechutra,
dehikah lechalba,
denashach leshunra
de'achla legadya
dizabin aba bitrei zuzei,
chad gadya, chad gadya.

Va'ata hashochet,
veshachat letora,
deshatah lemaya,
dekavah lenura,
desaraf lechutra,
dehikah lechalba,
denashach leshunra
de'achla legadya
dizabin aba bitrei zuzei,
chad gadya, chad gadya.

Then came the Angel of Death
and killed the slaughterer,
that slaughtered the ox,
that drank the water,
that quenched the fire,
that burnt the stick,
that beat the dog,
that bit the cat,
that ate the goat,
that Father bought for two zuzim,
Chad gadya, chad gadya.

Va'ata mal'ach hamavet,
veshachat leshochet,
deshachat letora,
deshatah lemaya,
dekavah lenura,
desaraf lechutra,
dehikah lechalba,
denashach leshunra
de'achla legadya
dizabin aba bitrei zuzei,
chad gadya, chad gadya.

Then came the Holy One, Blessed
be He
and slew the the Angel of Death,
that killed the slaughterer,
that slaughtered the ox,
that drank the water,
that quenched the fire,
that burnt the stick,
that beat the dog,
that bit the cat,
that ate the goat,
that Father bought for two zuzim,
Chad gadya, chad gadya.

Va'ata HaKadosh
Baruch-Hu,
veshachat lemal'ach hamavet,
deshachat leshochet,
deshachat letora,
deshatah lemaya,
dekavah lenura,
desaraf lechutra,
dehikah lechalba,
denashach leshunra
de'achla legadya
dizabin aba bitrei zuzei,
chad gadya, chad gadya.

WHO KNOWS ONE
(ECHAD MI YODEA)

Who knows one? I know one!
One is our God in the Heaven and the Earth.

Who knows two? I know two! Two are the tablets that Moses brought.
One is our God in the Heaven and the Earth.

Who knows three? I know three!
Three are the patriarchs.
Two are the tablets that Moses brought.
One is our God in the Heaven and the Earth.

Who knows …

Four are the matriarchs.
Five are the books of the (clap) Torah...
Six are orders of the (clap) Mishnah...
Seven are the days of the week (clap clap)...
Eight are the days before a baby's bris...
Nine are the months of childbirth…
Ten are the commandments...
Eleven are the stars in Joseph's dream...
Twelve are the tribes of Israel...
Thirteen are the attributes of God.

Echad mi yode'a? Echad ani yode'a: echad Eloheinu shebashamayim u'va'aretz.

אֶחָד מִי יוֹדֵעַ? אֶחָד אֲנִי יוֹדֵעַ:
אֶחָד אֱלֹהֵינוּ שֶׁבַּשָּׁמַיִם וּבָאָרֶץ.

Shnayim mi yode'a? Shnayim ani yode'a:
shnai luchot habrit,
echad Eloheinu shebashamayim u'va'aretz.

שְׁנַיִם מִי יוֹדֵעַ? שְׁנַיִם אֲנִי יוֹדֵעַ:
שְׁנֵי לֻחוֹת הַבְּרִית.
אֶחָד אֱלֹהֵינוּ שֶׁבַּשָּׁמַיִם וּבָאָרֶץ.

Shloshah mi yode'a? Shloshah ani yode'a:
shloshah avot,
shnai luchot habrit,
echad Eloheinu shebashamayim u'va'aretz.

שְׁלֹשָׁה מִי יוֹדֵעַ? שְׁלֹשָׁה אֲנִי יוֹדֵעַ:
שְׁלֹשָׁה אָבוֹת,
שְׁנֵי לֻחוֹת הַבְּרִית,
אֶחָד אֱלֹהֵינוּ שֶׁבַּשָּׁמַיִם וּבָאָרֶץ.

Arba mi yode'a? Arba ani yode'a:

אַרְבַּע מִי יוֹדֵעַ? אַרְבַּע אֲנִי יוֹדֵעַ:

arba imahot
chamishah chumshei Torah...
shishah sidrei mishnah...
shiv'ah yimei shabbata...
 shmonah yimei milah...
tishah yarchai laidah...
asarah dibraiya...
echad asar kochvaya...
shnaim asar shivtaiya...
shloshah asar midaiya.

אַרְבַּע אִמָּהוֹת
חֲמִשָּׁה חוּמְשֵׁי תוֹרָה
שִׁשָּׁה סִדְרֵי מִשְׁנָה
שִׁבְעָה יְמֵי שַׁבָּתָא
שְׁמוֹנָה יְמֵי מִילָה
תִּשְׁעָה יַרְחֵי לֵדָה
עֲשָׂרָה דִבְּרַיָּא
אַחַד עָשָׂר כּוֹכְבַיָּא
שְׁנֵים עָשָׂר שִׁבְטַיָּא
שְׁלֹשָׁה עָשָׂר מִדַּיָּא

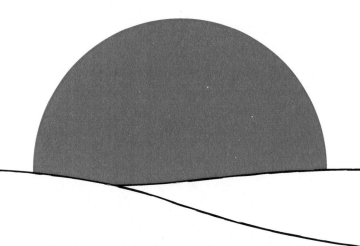

ACKNOWLEDGMENTS

RABBINIC CONSULTANTS:

*Thank you to **Sari Laufer** who served as a rabbinic consultant on this project. She is a rabbi at Stephen Wise Temple in Los Angeles, where she is the Director of Congregational Engagement. She lives in L.A. with her husband and children.*

*Additional rabbinic consulting provided by **Rabbi Joshua Cahan**, who teaches Rabbinics and Tefillah at Solomon Schechter School of Westchester. He holds a PhD in Talmud from the Jewish Theological Seminary, and edited a popular bencher (book of Shabbat songs and blessings), "Yedid Nefesh."*

SPECIAL THANKS TO:

Rabbi Dan Ain, Alana Ain, Lisa Keys, Deborah Kolben, and the staff at 70 Faces Media. The following sources were especially helpful in the creation of this haggadah: Sefaria, Haggadot.com, Robert Alter, Chabad.org and My Jewish Learning.

Kveller is a website and online community of women and parents who want to add a bit of Jewish flavor to their lives, their parenting, and their world. From trying to conceive to finding balance, and from celebrating holidays to planning a bat mitzvah, we're here to inspire you and empathize with you, every step along the way. Kveller is published by 70 Faces Media.

CREATORS OF THIS PROJECT

ELISSA STRAUSS

Elissa is a writer and essayist whose work has appeared in the New York Times, Glamour, ELLE, and elsewhere. She's covered parenthood for Slate.com and CNN.com, where she writes the advice column, "Am I a Bad Parent?" From 2013 to 2017, she was the co-artistic director of LABA: A Laboratory for New Jewish Culture in New York. She lives in the Bay Area with her husband and two sons.

GABRIELLE BIRKNER

Gabrielle is a writer, editor, and the co-author of "Modern Loss: Candid Conversation About Grief. Beginners Welcome" (Harper Wave, 2018). Her work has appeared in the Wall Street Journal, the New York Times, the Cut, Vice, and many other publications. She served previously as managing editor of JTA and digital director at the Forward. Gabrielle lives in Los Angeles with her husband and children.

HANE GRACE YAGEL

Grace is the Multimedia Editor at 70 Faces Media. She was born in New York to Israeli parents, and moved back to Israel with her family when she was 7 years old. She received her B.Design in Visual Communications in 2016, and has since moved to New York, where she has worked on many graphic design, video, and other visual content projects.

This project was made possible with support from the Diane P. and Guilford Glazer Fund of the Jewish Community Foundation of Los Angeles.